Off Coldwater Canyon

C.W. Emerson

Third Place Winner of The Poetry Box Chapbook Prize 2020

Poems ©2021 C.W. Emerson
All rights reserved.

Editing, Book & Cover Design: Shawn Aveningo Sanders
Cover Photo: Pawel Czerwinski
Author photo: Nasim Saleh

No part of this book may be reproduced in any manner whatsoever without permission from the author, except in the case of brief quotations embodied in critical essays, reviews and articles.

ISBN: 978-1-948461-73-3
Printed in the United States of America.
Wholesale Distribution via Ingram.

Published by The Poetry Box®, 2021
Portland, Oregon
ThePoetryBox.com

*I let myself dry like a dandelion.
When all but my stem had vanished,
with nothing left to be blown away,
finally, I was free.*

Contents

How I Came To Be Myself   7

༄

Prologue   11
The Impossible Time   12
Coldwater Canyon Suite
    i. Off Coldwater Canyon, 1982   14
    ii. Aftermath, 1985   21
    iii. Reclamation, 1987   25
Afterword   29
Epilogue   30

༄

Acknowledgments   33
Praise for *Off Coldwater Canyon*   35
About the Author   37
The Poetry Box® Chapbook Prize   38

How I Came To Be Myself

~after Justin Boening, "How I Came to Rule the World"

You remind me of myself
at twenty-five:
              electrified,
& living off stars
that fell into my hair, my eyes—

              like you,
I dreamt of infernos, fields
deliberately set aflame—
              fires kindled
by bursts of atoms
culled from summer storms.

On the morning of my milestone day
I scaled the city walls, breathed
the unbreathable city air

(the fields,
       in my nightmares,
              blazing, blazing . . .)

& for crimes committed
or any conceived,
        I declared my absolution.

I knew that, soon, they would come for me.

I armed the doors & the paintings,
stared at my own battered face.

[. . .]

I let myself dry like a dandelion.

When all but my stem had vanished,
with nothing left   to be blown away,

    finally,   I was free.

The rest, as they say, is the rest.

Prologue

Didn't I stand there once,
nineteen, loose-limbed,

dripping water onto the catwalk
above the motel pool?

And weren't we luminous then?—
our bodies glistening,

pale as the slice of winter moon
that hung in a Vegas sky.

Wasn't there a door, a threshold,
one simple, white-walled room?

You'd have become
bobcat, eucalyptus, salt cedar,
my love—

had you lived a little longer.

The Impossible Time

I was falling in love with the world, and everything in the world was dying.

There was no end to what threatened us. I sheltered under leaves, in the dark humus. I waited for it to be over, but it was never over. There would be no future, so we made no plans.

Still, the air had a sweetness and tang; we were young, the lines of our bodies light and lithe, the night air filled with valley jasmine, with smoke from deep in the Tenderloin, with traces of champagne wafting over Brooklyn's snow-clad streets.

That winter, our breath misted the windows of my old Chevy, your new coupe. I was in love with the thought of you. But you were already gone.

∞

The leaves and the bodies kept falling around me. I tracked the snowpack as it melted, focused my gaze on the ground below—or did it happen in another way entirely?—in a time of such impossibilities, what exactly is the truth? A narrator soaked in hardscrabble gin, a bulletproof screen that kicks our bullets back at us.

It happened in broken nights littered with fever and sweat-soaked sheets that signaled our imminent demise. There was no escaping death's widening presence. But even so, we would not die.

❧

For years I floated above the carnage, then finally rejoined the herd of the living—cleaned out closets, made arrangements, moved through the necessary days. The faces and place-names bent and merged into something that felt like safety. I shadowed the plague from seaboard to seaboard, marched up Fifth Avenue flanked by stars and suffragettes, slunk down Sunset Boulevard with wreckage like me from the streets and alleys.

❧

One morning, I woke to a clear sky flocked with white, a dusting of feathers over the Hudson Valley. I prayed that something of our kind would find its way into time's pleats and waves—our grace and beauty, the way we defied expectations of weakness—that despite our decimation, we would endure.

This was how life came back to me, afterward—the way light filters through bamboo shades, insinuates itself, then disperses the night. The planets in their new configurations, a subtle shifting of the elements. Time, its planes like sheets of glass: sharp, translucent, slicing the air.

Coldwater Canyon Suite

i. Off Coldwater Canyon, 1982

I was nineteen
when I stepped off the plane
            that had carried me
from Rochester to L.A.,

away from my father's pronouncements
of what made a man a man,
a life worth living—

just beyond baggage claim
and the hiss
of the electric doors,
            that first blast
of carbon-fueled, dream-filled air

melted the frosted past, quelled
my rising panic, rearranged
the way light fell forever.

                ☙

I don't remember driving
to North Hollywood that first morning;
but just off Coldwater Canyon
I discovered a place called *The Riverton Arms*—

apartments linked
by manicured walkways, artfully lit—
which seemed, to me,
            the height of refinement—

a magical compound,
where men loved men and fountains flowed,
and greens exploded into fire-blossom;

where scents of pine and rosemary
mingled and baked in the slow valley days,
and ambient freeway
                white noise lullabies
sang us into morning's smog-soaked light.

༄

Little Sam lived with Roberto,
           and Big Sam with Bob
in a haze of good taste and Italian cologne.

Big Sam wore his moustache
thick and lush,
exactly like the Marlboro Man.

Roberto was covered
with tattoos and piercings,
a pirate on the prowl.

Bob could have been a model for *Colt*,
with his feathered hair and chiseled jaw.

And Little Sam's smile
            was unabashed joy—
a boy from the streets of east L.A.,
sheltered by lindens and sycamores
lining both sides of Riverton Drive.

I took a studio in the back,
furnished the place with one twin bed,
microphones, cables, electric piano—

[. . .]

spent my days composing songs,
making demos on a two-track reel-to-reel,

imagined them on the radio,
my name rising high on the Billboard charts.

For now, my music
seeped through walls
                and flowed over walkways,
letting neighbors know I was home.

                ◦◦

Nights and weekends
I worked at The Hayloft
                up on the boulevard
for minimum wage, plus tips and beer,

serving drinks
to the exquisite sweat-slicked men
                sliding up to the bar
straight off the dance floor.

They traveled in packs, *these golden ones*,
and came for the reasons
                they'd always come:
to revel, to dream,
to dance away the night—

to see their own reflections
                glitter and gleam
under the blaze of the dance floor lights.

After hours, men would embrace
in darkened corners of the bar,

drinking shots, making toasts
to hopes and ambitions
long forgotten by morning.

❦

For two years, I hustled drinks;
every night, shirtless dancers
swayed to the beat.

One morning in early winter,
upon the scrim of muscle and rib—
   skin that had always been smooth, unblemished—
there, on the naked back of a dancer,
the faintest trace of lavender arose.

When torsos flowered
with fields of purple lesions,
the dancers cleared the dance floor,
            whispered goodbye
to their carefully imagined futures:

to the big house
            in the Hollywood Hills
with the perfect companion,

to the good job
with good insurance
they wouldn't live long enough to use.

❦

The men at *The Riverton Arms*
            grew fragile, weary,
holding on to old grudges
as they nursed one another—

[. . .]

more companions
than fervent lovers.

Big Sam made plans to leave L.A.,
headed for the vast northwest.

Roberto's legs would buckle
every time he tried to leave his bed.

☙

Roberto and Little Sam
had bedrooms that adjoined;
I seemed to be always
             with one or the other
all that winter and into the spring,
doling out medications,
making up beds for visiting family,

walking alone in the April rain
to Henry's Tacos
             for take-out burritos
in grease-soaked paper bags.

And every afternoon,
once the boys were asleep,
Bob and I would steal away,
out to my old Impala—

with the ragtop down
          and the radio cranked,
we'd haul ass the length of the 101,

stopping to check on our bedridden friends:
delivering meals they would rarely eat,
changing the dampened linens,

checking for rashes, fever spikes,
and touching them—

        always, we touched them—

we'd rub their calloused feet,
hold withered hands

gone cold, so often,
        in the afternoon heat.

        ⚘

One sweltering August morning
in a bare-bones church in Eagle Rock,
just northeast of downtown L.A.,

Bob and I laid Little Sam to rest
in a simple wooden box.

In my pocket, a tiny keepsake urn—
a tablespoon of Roberto's ashes.

Little Sam had been twenty,
younger than I was.

His family was gathered
at the front of the church
where he lay, serene,
        in an open casket—

his father, drunk, as always,
his mother numb,
        her expression blank;

his teen-aged brothers, Peter and Paul,
trouble in matching leather jackets,

[. . .]

and his sister, Amelia,
elegant in black silk crepe,
a single strand of pearls.

The Catholic Mass droned on and on.

I handed the urn to Amelia.
She would sprinkle the ashes
                on her brother's coffin,
later, graveside at Forest Lawn.

I left before the final prayers,
gave no condolences,
                said no goodbyes.

I walked outside to my red Impala,
drove east along the 134
with no destination in mind.

There was no one
who needed attending to,

no reason not to drive on.

ii. Aftermath, 1985

To a man, they were gone,
my brothers-in-arms,
my lovers, my friends—

      massacred is not too strong a word—

first Rick and Roger,
              then Paco, Danny;

Jason, who had died alone—
he lay dead in the house
         on his Chatsworth ranch
two full days before anyone knew.

Little Sam was the last to go.
It seemed to me that a chapter had closed.

It was time to be finished
            with grief, self-pity,
time to relinquish my rosary of ashes—

time for my life to be something more
than an endless novena,
            a desperate prayer.

God wasn't listening anyway.

I was twenty-two and already old.

                ☙

I'd spent three years at *The Riverton Arms,*

      —that dreamlike place,
set apart from the world,

[. . .]

redolent with the scent of wild herbs
            and cultivated flowers.

Day after day,
I would drink in that magical western light,
breathe the smog that burnished it,

forgive the city
              a hundred times over
its indifference
to my star-struck dreams.

But that seemed a hundred years ago.

❦

Of the men I'd known at *The Riverton*,
only Bob and I remained—

Bob said he needed distance
now that Little Sam was gone.

I watched as he packed and drove away.

I did the things I needed to do:
emptied cupboards,
            bleached the linens,
plunged my hands into scalding water
laced with ammonia,

trying to scrub away
            the blood, the sorrow.

❦

The city's radiance was muted,
the lights on the boulevard dimmed.

I sat on a barstool at the Hayloft,
observed the swagger of
         my young replacement
as he served me tequila and cold Coronas,
everything *on the house.*

Men were filing into the bar
in smaller groups of two or three;
         actors, models, workaday fellows—

they came from offices, clothing stores,
they tracked in the dust
         of construction sites,
or had crawled out of bed at cocktail time.

Some came alone,
wearing denim, leather,
and cautious, wary smiles;

none of them knew if his latest lover
might be the next to fall.

There were still no explanations,
there was no plan, no protocol.

There was nothing to believe in,
nothing and no one to rally behind—

only a new suspicion of strangers,
the fear of contagion, the downcast eyes—
the abiding signs
         of incipient plague.

༄

Hundreds marched
in New York that summer, 1986.

[. . .]

Thousands were sick
in the desiccated south
and throughout the scorched Midwest.

Hollywood wept,
or pretended to weep—
        even then, it seemed to glisten.

I'd lie awake
with the windows open,
the summer night silent as smoke.

I wanted some reminder of paradise—

a whisper of breeze
        coming down from the canyon,
a note of jasmine in the evening air.

iii. Reclamation, 1987

Seven months after Bob packed up
        and left *The Riverton Arms*,
I moved a few miles up the road
from just off Coldwater Canyon
        to the flats of Van Nuys,

settled into a tiny duplex
lodged in a grove of eucalyptus
tucked away on Valerio Street.

Mornings I'd drive
        along Magnolia Boulevard,
stop for breakfast at Four and 20 Pies,

go to the nine o'clock AA meeting
for lack of anything better to do.

The coolness of fall was coming on;
autumn was lifting
        the dome of smog
that had covered the valley all summer.

By late September,
my money was dwindling—
but I was well, unlike so many others,
and I could work.

I took a job as a caregiver,
        unafraid of becoming ill
from simple, human contact.

Besides, I knew what the role required;
I'd seen men through their final days.

[. . .]

I seemed to know instinctively
how to care for my stricken friends—

what I didn't know
I learned from the hospice workers,
middle-aged women with careworn faces,
men with Mohawks, nose-rings,
                        and coal-black eyes.

But I wasn't prepared to care for strangers—
their eyes were foreign, suffused with fear,
unsettling, unfamiliar.

Each time I touched their bodies
my own revulsion shamed me,
      and every ministration—

swabbing away their acrid sweat,
soothing their lesions with herbal balms—
           left me drained, exhausted,
as though I were the one in need of care.

In the beating of their weakened hearts
was a hunger, an eagerness to live;

but I stood there at their bedsides—
                frozen, helpless,
lacking the will to go on:

      —for these were not the men I'd loved.

After a month, I gave notice,
                went home,

sat alone, outside in the garden.

I gave no thought to what might come next.
I was too numb to think,
                too beaten down,
fatigued beyond anything I could have imagined;

      I hadn't known a person could be so tired.

I sat among the eucalyptus,
their long, plaited leaves
                    perfuming the air
with mint and citronella—

a scent so bracing
it cut straight through the mid-day heat.

That boy who'd stepped off a plane in L.A.
was only a distant memory.

I was twenty-four,
and all but convinced
the best part of my life was over.

I'd long since set my music aside—
my own ambitions disappearing
                    the day I saw,
on the skin of a friend,
those first purple lesions.

I bought myself a real piano,
a second-hand Baldwin upright;

for the first time
           since the carnage began,
I played again, and composed—

[. . .]

odes to L.A., inconsolable city:
to days of blue sky powdered with cloud,
    and nights that blazed
      with klieg lights, jasmine;

love songs to the men we'd lost,
and the ones we had yet to lose—

innocent songs
for the boy I'd been,

psalms
for the heartbroken man I'd become.

I found something like hope
alive in the music,

something like freedom
urging me on.

Afterword

What I want you to know is that I did not survive. I want to tell you how the summer froze over, how I settled into the cottage, the one at the lake, told my family I had claimed it and would find a way to repay them later.

The snow fell in fragments. The old roan mare down on Poplar Beach didn't make it through the winter.

I want you to know that nothing happened to me all those years because I was not there, was not a person, did not exist. I was not anyone. My body endured, but I did not survive.

My father's rifle is there above the fireplace, your black parka on its hook by the door. Take them down; let's walk together. The ice is green and solid out beyond the pier.

Epilogue

For memory,
the sweet burnt rose
of holy wood—

Praise Robert, first to fall,
and Joey, splendid
in his yellow Corvette.

Praise Michael and Pierre
and the great open rooms
of their hearts.

Praise young Jason,
dead or alive,
for his soft surrender
and spine of steel.

Praise Roberto,
praise Louis,
who chose their burial wood
to match their chestnut eyes.

Praise memory.
Praise love
in all its mystery.

Help me remember what I am:

smoke and resin,
memory's ember.

Ash of the holy rose.

Acknowledgments

These poems first appeared in the following print and online journals:

The American Journal of Poetry: "Coldwater Canyon Suite"

The Comstock Review: "Afterword"

Mantis: "The Impossible Time"

New Ohio Review: "Prologue" (as "Stopover on a Road Trip to L.A., 1981")

Praise for
Off Coldwater Canyon

Tender is the word I thought of while reading *Off Coldwater Canyon*. This is the story of a young man, a paradise he found, and how that paradise—the gay community of Los Angeles in the early '80s—was destroyed by the AIDS epidemic. Emerson's poetry is so honest, its narrative so clear, that his compassion runs through every line: in the care he gave to his dying friends, the comfort he later tried to offer as a caregiver for strangers, and the blunt descriptions of the hollow aftermath and long road to recovery. This is a big-hearted poet, and a book that remembers and doesn't look away.

—Amy Miller, Contest Judge, 2020
and author of *The Trouble with New England Girls*

In this breathtakingly beautiful, heartbreakingly personal elegy to friends and lovers lost in the early days of the AIDS epidemic, C.W. Emerson maps a journey from innocence hungry for experience to experience hungry for lost innocence. *Off Coldwater Canyon* is not only an elegy to all those men who died too soon, but to a whole lost world of sensuality, possibility, daring. And if there's no way back to that particular world, Emerson ends his suite of poems with a path that opens toward another.

—Cecilia Woloch
author of *Tsigan: The Gypsy Poem*

The radiant from which *Off Coldwater Canyon* emanates is the body's own perishable luminosity, these poems the lyric

[. . .]

record of the body's trajectory as a falling star—meteoric, brief—during the height of the AIDs pandemic: While these poems possess the power to make a reader weep, Emerson, himself, never succumbs to a poet's vainest temptation: to eulogize mourning. Instead, Emerson dignifies the paths of those who have crisscrossed his own with a limpid accuracy that pinpoints and transpierces the essence of our fleeting existence and names it, a quality that destines this collection to become a classic in league with Thom Gunn's *The Man with Night Sweats*.

—Lise Goett, author of *Leprosarium*

About the Author

Poet and psychologist C.W. Emerson, raised in western New York's Finger Lakes region, now lives and works in Palm Springs, California. Following a varied, non-traditional career path as musician, celebrity assistant, and fundraising executive for The American Foundation for AIDS Research (Amfar), Emerson received his Ph.D. in Clinical Psychology from Fielding Graduate Institute in 2007.

C.W. Emerson is the recipient of the C. P. Cavafy Poetry Prize, as well as awards and honors from *The Atlanta Review, The Comstock Review, New Letters Press,* and others. His work has appeared in journals including *Crab Orchard Review, Greensboro Review, december, New Ohio Review,* and *The New Guard. Off Coldwater Canyon* is his first published chapbook.

The Poetry Box Chapbook Prize

In 2018, The Poetry Box® introduced their annual Chapbook Prize competition. The contest is open to both established poets and emerging talent alike, and the editors reserve the right to select more than one poet's manuscript for publication. Currently, the contest is open to poets residing in the United States and is open for submissions each year during the month of February. Find more information at ThePoetryBox.com.

2020 Winners:
The Day of My First Driving Lesson by Tiel Aisha Ansari
My Mother Never Died Before by Marcia B. Loughran
Off Coldwater Canyon by C.W. Emerson

2019 Winners:
Moroccan Holiday by Lauren Tivey
Hello, Darling by Christine Higgins
Falling into the River by Debbie Hall

2018 Winners:
Shrinking Bones by Judy K. Mosher
November Quilt by Penelope Scambly Schott
14: Antología del Sonoran by Christopher Bogart
Fireweed by Gudrun Bortman

www.ingramcontent.com/pod-product-compliance
Lightning Source LLC
LaVergne TN
LVHW040203080526
838202LV00042B/3304